Unit 4

HOUGHTON MIFFLIN HARCOURT
School Publishers

Contents

Go, Jones!

by Trey Barney

illustrated by Linda Chesak-Liberace

Jones woke up. It was time to
go, go, go! Jones will get Mike.

Mike had a bone.

"This bone is just for Jones," said Mike. "It is just for him."

Jones ran to get his bone. Jones
ran around and around. Then Jones
went to dig in the sand.

Jones dug a big hole. What will go in this big hole? The bone that Mike gave Jones will go in it.

But look! A big, big bone is in
the hole! It is such a big bone.

Can Jones dig it up? Can Jones
carry it?

Jones went home to get Mike
because the bone was so, so big.
Mike can help Jones dig it up.

Jones ran and got Mike. Mike
dug and dug. So did Jones. Jones
rode home with the big, big bone.

What can that big, big bone be?

So Much Fun

by Rosarita Mencia
illustrated by Diana Schoenbrun

Before the sun rose, Jack got on his bike. Jack rode and rode.

Jack rode his bike to Dan's home.
Jack had a note for Dan. Jack put
tape on his note and stuck it up.

Dan woke up. Dan put on his
robe. Dan got Jack's note. Then
Dan went back in with his note.

Meg woke up. Meg put on her robe. Meg got Jack's note. Then Meg went back in with her note.

Mo woke up. Mo put on his robe.
Mo got Jack's note. Then Mo went
back in with his note.

Mo,

Go to Big Pond.
Get to the pond
before 9:00.

Bring snacks.

Jack

Dan, Meg, and Mo sat. Jack got
up. Jack spoke.

"I will tell a joke," said Jack.

"Let's hope it is funny," said Mo.

Jack had so much fun telling jokes!
So did Dan. So did Meg. So did Mo.

18

June's Pictures

by Jolene Odegaard

June likes to take pictures.
It is so much fun. Click, click, click.

June likes those little pigs.
She thinks the pigs are so cute!
Click, click, click.

Six cute dogs sit on steps. June likes dogs. Click, click, click.

Cats are cute when they nap.
Cats doze a lot! June likes cats.
Click, click, click.

That gull stands on a pole.
June likes gulls and sand dunes.
Click, click, click.

That mule is standing in a nice pose. June likes mules. Click, click, click.

The ducks have soft white plumes.
June likes ducks. Click, click, click.

Bruce has a nice smile. Click. June will show Bruce this picture. June hopes Bruce will like it. Do you think he will?

My Mule, Duke

by Richard Stemple

illustrated by
Jackie Snider

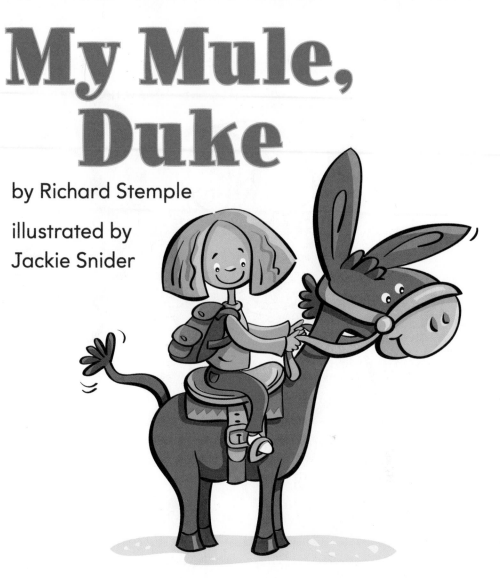

Duke is a big mule. Duke is a huge mule. Duke lets June ride on his back.

June is light. It is fun to sit on
Duke's back. Duke will carry June
home. They go clip, clop, clip, clop.

No! No! Duke sits down! June must go home. Get up! Be a good mule, Duke. Get up! Duke just sits.

What can June do? Duke just
sits. June must go home. Duke sits
still. Duke will not get up. June lets
Duke sit. June picks up the flute.

June can skip home. Skip, skip, skip. June can hop home. Hop, hop, hop. June can use the flute. June makes a tune.

June will play a tune. June skips
to the tune. June hops to the tune.
Skip, hop, hop, skip, hop, hop.
June skips and hops to the tune.

Duke likes June's tune. Duke gets
up. Duke runs, clip, clop, clop, to
June. Duke runs, clip, clop, clop, to
the tune. Clip, clop, clip, clop.

June will play the flute. Duke likes June's tune. Duke will carry June home. Clip, clop, clop. Clip, clop, clop.

At the Beach

by Elaine Sciofus
illustrated by David Sheldon

Pete is my best pal. We meet at the beach each week. We run and jump and yell. It's fun!

Pete is six. So am I. Pete has a
green cap. My hat is green. We eat
sweet peaches at the beach. Yum,
yum, yum.

Then we take a walk. Pete and I
hunt for shells. We keep about five
shells each.

Then we sit by the sea. Pete gets his feet wet. My feet get wet, too. Splash, splash, splash! We don't go in the sea. It's fun to just get wet feet.

We dig holes. Dig, dig, dig! The
sea runs in them. The holes fill up
fast. We get wet sand.

We get a lot of wet sand. We
make a neat sand beast.

The sand beast is like an eel.
Maybe it's a snake! We run and
jump over it.

Then Pete has to go home. So
do I. We had lots of fun. We will
meet at the beach next week.

Who Will Teach Us?

by Forest Von Gront

Mom is teaching Beth about planting seeds. Beth makes holes. She plants seeds. Beth will water the seeds and see them grow.

Miss Kim is teaching Lin a tune.
Each week Lin meets with Miss Kim.
Lin can read each note. She can play
well.

Dad is teaching Sam how to swim.
Dad is holding Sam while he kicks his
feet. Sam will be so glad when he
can swim.

Bob likes to teach kids how to play this game. He meets with them each week. He teaches them to use their feet and kick.

Mom is teaching Reed and Pete how to bake. She will teach them to be safe. She is helping them place drops on the sheet.

Nell's mom is teaching Nell how
to clean the car. Nell wipes it with a
mitt. Nell will clean it so it shines.

Gramps is teaching Bill about fishing. Bill can hold his fishing pole just like Gramps. Gramps tells Bill to be still when fish are close.

Could you teach a friend? What could you teach?

Plunk, Plunk

by Charles Barker
illustrated by Karen Stormer Brooks

Plunk, plunk! Drop, drop! Drops fall on Frank's cheek. What made those drops?

The drops got big. Plunk, plunk. Did Frank see what made those drops? No, but Frank did see a hint.

A green hose is in the green grass. Frank thinks it made the drops. He is sure it did.

The green hose leads Frank to this big tree trunk.

"Who is back there? I think it's Jean. Is it? Is it Jean?" asks Frank.

"Yes, Frank. It's me. Did you get wet?" asks Jean. "I hope you think it was fun."

"It was fun," Frank tells Jean.
"Will you help me rake? We can
sing as we rake. Rake, rake, rake.
Sing, sing, sing."

"Which song will we sing?"
Jean asks.

"Let's make up a song!
Ink-a-dink-a-dee!" sings Frank.
"Sing with me!"

"Helping you is fun," Jean tells
Frank, "and it's fun to sing!"

"Ink-a-dink-a-thanks!" Frank sings.

The King's Song

by Clint Moscari
illustrated by Valerie Sokolova

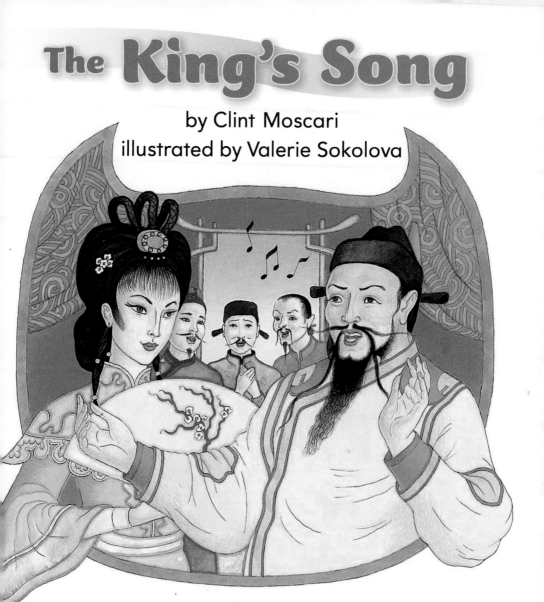

"Singing is my best thing," said
King Ming. He sang to Queen Ling.
He sang sweet tunes.

At five, Queen Ling sat. King
Ming got set to sing his song, but no
tune came out. King Ming did not
sing his song.

"Don't be sad, King Ming," said
Queen Ling. "Maybe a bird can help
you sing." Queen Ling wrote this
note: Needed: Bird that can teach King
Ming to sing.

Red Bird came, but he had no
songs. Pink Bird came, but he had
no songs.

Then Green Bird came. He had
sweet, sweet songs. His songs made
King Ming and Queen Ling smile.
Then Queen Ling spoke.

"King Ming has lost his song. Can
you teach King Ming to sing?" asked
Queen Ling.

"I think I can teach him as quick
as a wink," said Green Bird.

"I will bring him sweet notes
each time I come," said Green Bird.

In just a week, King Ming had his song back.

"Singing is my best thing," sang King Ming.

Ray Trains Dex

by Angie Tubbman
illustrated by Shirley Beckes

"Sit," Ray tells Dex. Dex sits.
"Good dog!"

"Stay," Ray tells Dex.

At first Dex stays. He stays and waits when Ray tells him.

But then, Dex will not sit and
wait. He runs.

Dex runs fast. Ray and Dad run
as fast as Dex.

"Stop, Dex," yells Ray. "Sit! Sit!"
Dex sits and waits.

"I think I hear a dog whine," Dad tells Ray. "Maybe it needs help."

"Go," Ray tells Dex. Dex runs. So do Ray and Dad.

Dex sees a dog. The dog's tail is
going thump, thump. She is glad to
see Dex. Dex sniffs, sniffs, sniffs.

"This dog has a cut," Dad tells
Ray. "It is not a bad cut."

Ray sees a rock on the ground.

"I think she got cut on this rock.
Do you think so, Dad?" asks Ray.

Dad nods as he checks the cut.

Call Kay if you
find this dog.
555-1234

"She is not a stray dog," Dad tells
Ray. "She has a tag. We will get
her food. Then we will call and tell
Kay to get her dog."

Sweet Treats

by Cyrus Rutherman

Grapes are a sweet treat. These kids like to snack on grapes every day. Would you like a bunch right now?

Grapes grow on big vines.
Grapes can be green. Grapes can
be red, deep blue, and black.

Lines and lines of grape plants grow in the ground. Grape plants need sun. Grape plants need rain.

Grapes stay on vines a long time. After a wait, grapes will be ripe. Grapes take time to get big and plump and sweet.

Ripe grapes cannot stay on vines. Ripe grapes need to be picked when it is time. Ripe grapes must be picked by hand.

Trucks bring grapes to shops and stands. Fresh grapes cannot stay on trucks. Grapes may rot if they stay too long.

See the sweet fresh grapes at this stand. Which fresh grapes would you snack on?

Kay has a huge tray filled with fresh green grapes. She can't wait, so she takes a big bunch!

"Yum! Yum! Yum!"

What Will We Do?

by Mandy Jackson
illustrated by Nicole Wong

It's a hot, hot day. It is too hot to run and play. What can we do?

We'd like to swim, but we
can't. Bay Lake isn't open.
What'll we do if we can't swim?

We can't play on the deck.
It has wet paint. What'll we do
if we can't play on the deck?

We'll read! It'll be fun! Let's
sit and read!

This tale is the best. A big, bad
beast chases three nice pigs. It wails
and wails. It trails those pigs home.
It keeps on wailing and wailing!

Wait! That's not right! It
doesn't wail! It huffs and puffs!
Huff, huff, huff! Puff, puff, puff!

No, no, no! You must be
mixed up. Beasts don't huff
and puff. Beasts wail!

Well, sometimes beasts huff
and puff. This beast huffs and
puffs. This beast huffs and
puffs and chases YOU!

Let's Eat

by Robert Stewart
illustrated by John Segal

The day had ended. It was time to
eat. Nell had a plate filled with meat.
"It's time to get Ben," said Nell.
"He'd hate to be late."

While Nell was out, Fay came in.
Fay had a pot filled with rice. She
put rice on a plate.

"Nell likes rice and peas. She'll
like this," said Fay.

While Nell was out, Blaine came
in. Blaine had a pot filled with
beans. Blain put beans in a big dish.

"Ben likes beans. He'll like this,"
said Blaine.

Then Jess came in. Jess filled
each cup with grape drink.
"Nell likes grapes. She'll like this.
She will," said Jess

Nell and Ben came home.

"Isn't this a treat?" asked Ben.

"Yes, it is," said Nell. "I didn't make this, but I know who did."

Nell gave Ben a note.

Please come quick.
Let's have fun.
Your pals,
Nell and Ben

Nell set five gray plates and five red cups. Ben went and got Fay, Blaine, and Jess.

Nell, Ben, Fay, Blaine, and Jess had a fine meal.

"Let's clean up," said Jess.

Under each plate was a thank you note!

It Was Snow Fun

by Shira Alami

illustrated by Jamie Smith

Snow fell on the grass. Snow fell
on oak trees. Snow fell and fell.

Bill was sleeping when it snowed.
When he woke up the snow was
there. Bill got up fast. Bill likes
snow. He likes snow a lot.

Bill ran and woke up Joan. He
will show Joan the snow.

"Get up, Joan. Get up, get up!
It snowed, Joan!" said Bill.

Joan got up.

"We can get dressed and put on hats and coats. Then we can go and play in the snow," said Joan.

Bill fell in the snow on his back.
Joan fell in the snow, too. Bill made
snow wings. Bill and Joan had snow
all over them.

Bill made a little white snow cat.
Joan put a bow on it. It was cute.
"Can we make a snow dog,
Joan?" asked Bill when he was done.

"Not in this wind. It is blowing
the snow. We must go in. Quick.
Let's go!" said Joan.

"Yes," said Bill. "Let's go!"

"Did you have fun?" asked Mom.

"It was great when the wind didn't blow. Then it was snow fun!" said Bill. Joan just laughed.

Boat Rides

by Redmond Turner

Is it time for a ride? A boat ride can be so much fun.

This boat has sails as white as
snow. The big white sails make the
boat go. Wind blows and fills the
sails.

Strong winds can make the boat
go fast! It is fun to sail, but you
must stay safe. You need a life vest.

This flat boat has no sails. It is slow. You use a pole to make it float. It can carry loads down this stream.

This boat is a raft. It is fun to
ride fast on white waves. Hats and
life vests help keep this ride safe.

This boat has no sail. It is not a raft. To make this boat go you must row. If you stop rowing, the boat will just float and drift off.

This man rows with his left hand. Then he rows with his right hand. He will just keep rowing. Soon his boat will pick up speed.

This boat is a huge ship. It can take long trips at sea. If you were on this ship, you could eat, sleep, and play games on it. Would that be great?

Fun with Gram

by Frances Berry
illustrated by Judith Lanfredi

Joan can't wait to go to
Gram's. She knows it will be fun.
So far, they've cut rows of paper
dolls. What's next?

Gram and Joan have a nice
snack. Then Gram has a plan.
"Let's go," she tells Joan. "I
know where we can have fun!"

Gram shows Joan a huge, oak trunk. It's loaded with things. Joan sees coats and hats and a dress.

"Gram," she asks, "where did
you get this green silk dress?"
"It's from Pops. Put it on."
Gram and Joan laugh.

Gram's green dress is so soft.
The silk floats around Joan. Gram's
face glows. Joan looks nice.

Joan takes off the dress.
Then she sees a green silk hat.
She puts it on. It fits!

Mom and Rob come in.
Gram tells Rob to see what
Pops left in the trunk. Rob sees
a big tan hat and a gray vest.

"We're playing dress up!" Joan and Rob laugh. "When we're at Gram's, we know we'll have fun!"

Rex Knows

by Paul Russell

illustrated by Susan Lexa

"Wake up," Joan tells Rex. "It's
time for work."

Rex likes his job, so he gets up.

Joan fills each bowl.

"Eat up so you can do a great job," Joan hints as Rex eats.

"Stay still," laughs Joan. "Slow down. We've no time to play. I must brush your coat so it feels soft."

Then Joan gets her coat and the leash. Rex and Joan go to work. Joan knows that Rex likes his job so much! Joan likes it, too.

On the way, Rex sees Nat and his dog Duke. Nat knows that Rex can't stop to play. Nat knows Rex must get to his job on time.

Joan stops and talks with Kate.
"So, is it time for work, Rex?"
asks Kate. "Must Rex go?"
"Yes, we're on our way," Joan
tells Kate. "We'll have fun."

Joan and Rex get to work. Rex
sits still while Joan rings the bell.
Ring, ring, ring. Soon Rick lets
Joan and Rex in.

Rex is good at playing. He can
do tricks and make each friend smile.
Rex knows they're glad to see him.

Bedtime for Ray

by Tami Lo Verso
illustrated by Yvette Banek

It was bedtime. Ray didn't want
to go to bed yet. He wanted to play
his game. He wanted to win.

Ray is six. He can tell time. Ray's
dad has a rule about bedtime. On a
weekday, Ray's bedtime is at 8:00. It
was that time.

So Ray went up the steps.
Shep went with him. Shep likes to
be with Ray, and Ray likes to be
with Shep.

Shep likes to watch Ray. Shep
gets in the bathtub to see Ray brush
his teeth. Ray can't let Shep do that.
Shep can't be in the tub!

Ray must try to get Shep out. So Ray gets in the bathtub. Ray can't lift Shep up, but he gets Shep out. Shep grins as if it is a game.

At last, Ray gets in his bed. His mother reads him a nice bedtime tale. Shep is so big that he can't sleep on Ray's bed.

Shep can't get on Ray's bed, but Shep has a rug. Shep sleeps on the rug at Ray's bedside.

Ray's dream is about his game.
In his dream, Ray wins the game.
What do you think Shep's
dream is?

Pancake Ran

retold by George O'Neal
illustrated by Carol Koeller

At sunrise, Midge and Madge got
up. Midge and Madge made a big,
big pancake.

"This is just for me," said Midge.
"No, it is not," hissed Madge.
While Midge and Madge yelled,
Pancake jumped up.

Then Pancake ran out the door.
Midge and Madge ran after
Pancake. Midge and Madge did not
catch him.

Pancake ran down a hillside and met Sheep.

"I will catch you," boasted Sheep.

"Midge and Madge did not catch me," yelled Pancake as he ran. "You cannot catch me, Sheep."

Pancake ran past an old windmill and met Goat.

"I will catch you," grunted Goat.

"Midge, Madge, and Sheep did not catch me," yelled Pancake. "You can try, but you cannot catch me."

Pancake sat on the roadside
and rested.

"Where are you going?"
asked Fox.

"I am going on a trip," said
Pancake.

"I cannot hear you," said Fox.
"Get close."

But, Pancake just ran.

Then Pancake jumped on a
sailboat with big white sails. He
sailed and sailed and sailed.

A Springtime Rain

by Hilda Ramirez

We like rain. We are glad
when it rains. It's fun to be
out in a springtime rain.

Kay likes to walk her dog in the rain. Rain can wash pathways and make them clean.

Kay sees raindrops shine on plants. Rain helps plants grow and spread.

Dad takes Quinn to class.
Quinn is dressed for rain. He has
his raincoat. He has a matching
rain hat on his head.

Beth and Gwen are dressed for rain, too. Their mom watches as they head to school. Gwen holds Beth's hand.

When it rains a lot, we stay in. Swings and slides get wet, so we can't use them. We get a long playtime in class.

Jane peeks out. She sees raindrops on the glass. Jane looks up.

"Quick!" Jane yells. "You must see this!"

We see a huge rainbow!
The rainbow glows. Sunshine
is on its way.

Rosebud

by Mary Martinez
illustrated by Benrei Huang

My mother had a big white boat.
Mom's big white boat was an old
sailboat. Mom let me name it.

I chose "Rosebud." Mom got red paint and paintbrushes. We painted that name on the boat. I painted a red rosebud.

Mom and I went sailing. We
sailed in the daytime. On nice days,
we set sail at sunrise. Sometimes we
sailed all day long.

If it rained, we stayed inside the boat. We played games. We read. But sailing was more fun than being inside.

When the sun peeked out, we'd
go up and sit topside. The sailboat
rocked and we sang songs. We sang,
"Row, row, row your boat."

One time we went on a long trip.
We sailed and sailed. It was sunset,
but it was not bedtime yet.

The sun's rays spread. The sea
glowed yellow and red. Then no
more rays. The sun had set.

It was time to head to bed. It
was bedtime on Rosebud.

Word Lists

Accompanies
"Let's Go to the Moon"

Go, Jones!
page 3

Decodable Words
Target Skill: Long *o* (CV, CVC*e*)
bone, go, hole, home, Jones, rode, so, woke

Previously Taught Skills
and, big, but, can, did, dig, dug, gave, get, got, had, help, him, his, in, is, it, just, Mike, ran, sand, such, that, then, this, time, up, went, will, with

High-Frequency Words
New
around, because, carry

Previously Taught
a, be, for, look, said, the, to, was, what

So Much Fun
page 11

Decodable Words
Target Skill: Long *o* (CV, CVC*e*)
go, home, hope, joke, jokes, Mo, note, robe, rode, rose, so, spoke, woke

Previously Taught Skills
9:00, and, back, big, bike, Dan, Dan's, did, fun, get, got, had, his, in, is, it, Jack, Jack's, let's, Meg, much, on, pond, sat, snack, stuck, sun, tape, tell, telling, then, up, went, will, with

High-Frequency Words
New
before, bring

Previously Taught
a, for, funny, her, I, put, said, the, to

June's Pictures

page 19

Decodable Words
Target Skill: Long *u* (CVC*e*)
Bruce, cute, dunes, June, mule, mules, plumes

Target Skill: Long *o* (CV, CVC*e*)
doze, hopes, pole, pose, so, those

Previously Taught Skills
and, cats, click, dogs, ducks, fun, gull, gulls, has, in, is, it, like, likes, lot, much, nap, nice, on, pigs, sand, sit, six, smile, soft, standing, stands, steps, take, that, this, when, white, will

High-Frequency Words
New
show, think, thinks

Previously Taught
a, are, do, have, he, little, picture, pictures, she, the, they, to, you

My Mule, Duke

page 27

Decodable Words
Target Skill: Long *u* (CVC*e*)
Duke, Duke's, flute, huge, June, June's, mule, tune, use

Target Skill: Long *o* (CV, CVC*e*)
go, home, no

Previously Taught Skills
and, back, big, can, clip, clop, fun, get, gets, his, hop, hops, is, it, just, lets, likes, makes, must, not, on, picks, ride, runs, sit, sits, skip, skips, still, up, will

High-Frequency Words
New
carry, light

Previously Taught
a, be, do, down, good, play, the, they, to, what

At the Beach

page 35

Decodable Words
Target Skill: Long *e* (CV, CVC*e*) Vowel Pairs *ee, ea*

beach, beast, each, eat, eel, feet, green, keep, meet, neat, peaches, Pete, sea, sweet, we, week

Previously Taught Skills
am, an, and, at, best, cap, dig, fast, fill, five, fun, get, gets, go, had, has, hat, his, holes, home, hunt, in, is, it's, jump, just, like, lot, lots, make, next, pal, run, runs, sand, shells, sit, six, snake, so, splash, take, them, then, up, wet, will, yell, yum

High-Frequency Words
New
about, by, don't, maybe

Previously Taught
a, do, for, I, my, of, over, the, to, too, walk

Who Will Teach Us?

page 43

Decodable Words
Target Skill: Long *e* (CV, CVC*e*) Vowel Pairs *ee, ea*

be, clean, each, feet, he, meets, Pete, read, Reed, see, seeds, she, sheet, teach, teaches, teaching, week

Previously Taught Skills
and, bake, Beth, Bill, Bob, can, close, Dad, drops, fish, fishing, game, glad, Gramps, he, helping, his, holes, is, it, just, kick, kicks, kids, Kim, like, likes, Lin, makes, Miss, mitt, Mom, mom, Nell, Nell's, note, on, place, planting, plants, pole, safe, Sam, shines, so, still, swim, tells, them, this, tune, use, well, while, will, wipes, with

High-Frequency Words
New
about, car, could

Previously Taught
a, are, friend, grow, hold, holding, how, play, the, their, to, water, who, what, you

Plunk, Plunk

page 51

Decodable Words
Target Skill: Final *ng*, *nk*
dink, Frank, Frank's, ink, plunk, sing, sings, song, thanks, think, thinks, trunk

Target Skill: Long *e* (CV, CVC*e*) Vowel Pairs *ee*, *ea*
cheek, dee, green, he, Jean, leads, me, see, tree, we

Previously Taught Skills
and, as, asks, back, big, but, can, did, drop, drops, fun, get, grass, help, helping, hint, hope, hose, in, is, it, it's, let's, made, make, no, on, rake, tells, this, those, up, wet, which, will, with, yes

High-Frequency Words
New
sure, there

Previously Taught
a, fall, I, the, to, was, what, who, you

The King's Song

page 59

Decodable Words
Target Skill: Final *ng*, *nk*
bring, King, Ling, Ming, Pink, sang, sing, singing, song, songs, thing, think, wink

Target Skill: Long *e* (CV, CVC*e*) Vowel Pairs *ee*, *ea*
be, each, Green, he, needed, Queen, sweet, teach, week

Previously Taught Skills
and, as, asked, at, back, best, but, came, can, did, five, got, had, has, help, him, his, in, is, just, lost, made, no, not, note, notes, quick, Red, sad, sat, set, smile, spoke, that, then, this, time, tune, tunes, will, wrote

High-Frequency Words
New
don't, maybe

Previously Taught
a, bird, Bird, come I, my, out, said, to, you

Ray Trains Dex

page 67

Decodable Words
Target Skill: Vowel Pairs *ai*, *ay*
Kay, Ray, stay, stays, stray, tail, trains, wait, waits

Previously Taught Skills
555-1234, and, as, asks, at, bad, but, checks, cut, Dad, Dex, dog, dog's, fast, get, glad, go, going, got, has, he, help, him, if, is, it, needs, nods, not, on, rock, run, runs, see, sees, she, sit, sits, sniffs, so, stop, tag, tell, tells, then, think, this, thump, we, when, whine, will, yells

High-Frequency Words
New
first, food, ground

Previously Taught
a, call, do, find, good, hear, her, I, maybe, the, to, you

Sweet Treats

page 75

Decodable Words
Target Skill: Vowel Pairs *ai*, *ay*
day, Kay, may, rain, stay, tray, wait

Previously Taught Skills
and, at, be, big, black, bring, bunch, can, cannot, can't, deep, filled, fresh, get, grape, grapes, green, hand, has, huge, if, in, is, it, kids, like, lines, long, must, need, on, picked, plants, plump, red, ripe, rot, see, she, shops, snack, so, stand, stands, sun, sweet, take, takes, these, time, treat, trucks, vines, when, which, will, with, yum

High-Frequency Words
New
ground, right, these

Previously Taught
a, after, are, blue, by, every, grow, now, of, the, they, to, too, you, would

167

What Will We Do?

page 83

Decodable Words
Target Skill: Contractions *'ll, 'd*
it'll, we'd, we'll

Target Skill: Vowel Pairs *ai, ay*
Bay, day, paint, play, trails, wail, wailing, wails, wait

Previously Taught Skills
and, bad, be, beast, beasts, best, big, but, can, can't, chases, deck, fun, has, home, hot, huff, huffs, if, is, isn't, it, it's, keeps, Lake, let's, like, mixed, must, nice, no, not, on, pigs, puff, puffs, read, run, sit, swim, tale, that's, this, those, three, up, we, well, wet

High-Frequency Words
New
right, sometimes

Previously Taught
a, do, doesn't, don't, open, the, to, too, what, what'll, you

Let's Eat

page 91

Decodable Words
Target Skill: Contractions *'ll, 'd*
he'd, he'll, she'll

Target Skill: Vowel Pairs *ai, ay*
Blaine, day, Fay, gray

Previously Taught Skills
and, asked, be, beans, Ben, big, but, came, clean, cup, cups, did, didn't, dish, drink, each, eat, ended, filled, fine, five, fun, gave, get, got, grape, grapes, had, hate, home, in, is, isn't, it, it's, Jess, late, let's, like, likes, make, meal, meat, Nell, note, on, pals, peas, plate, plates, please, pot, quick, red, rice, set, she, thank, then, this, time, treat, up, went, while, will, with, yes

High-Frequency Words
New
under, your

Previously Taught
a, come, have, I, know, out, put, said, the, to, was, who, you

It Was Snow Fun

page 99

Decodable Words
Target Skill: Vowel Pairs *oa*, *ow*
blow, blowing, bow, coats, Joan, oak,
show, snow, snowed

Previously Taught Skills
and, asked, back, Bill, can, cat, cute, did,
didn't, dog, dressed, fast, fell, fun, get, go,
got, grass, had, hats, he, his, in, it, just,
let's, likes, lot, made, make, Mom, must,
not, on, play, quick, ran, sleeping, them,
then, this, trees, up, we, when, white,
will, wind, wings, woke, yes

High-Frequency Words
New
done, great, laugh

Previously Taught
a, all, have, little, over,
put, said, the, there, too,
was, you

Boat Rides

page 107

Decodable Words
Target Skill: Vowel Pairs *oa*, *ow*
blows, boat, float, loads, row, rowing,
rows, slow, snow

Previously Taught Skills
and, as, at, be, big, but, can, drift, eat, fast,
fills, flat, fun, games, go, hand, has, hats,
he, help, his, huge, if, is, it, just, keep,
left, life, make, man, much, must, need,
no, not, off, on, pick, play, pole, raft, ride,
safe, sail, sails, sea, ship, sleep, so, speed,
stay, stop, stream, strong, take, then, this,
time, trips, up, use, vest, vests, waves,
white, will, wind, winds, with

High-Frequency Words
New
great, soon, were

Previously Taught
a, carry, could, down, for,
right, the, to, would, you

169

Fun with Gram

page 115

Decodable Words
Target Skill: Contractions *'ve, 're*
we're

Target Skill: Vowel Pairs *oa, ow*
coats, floats, glows, Joan, know, knows,
loaded, oak, rows, shows

Previously Taught Skills
and, asks, at, be, big, can, can't, cut, did,
dolls, dress, face, fits, from, fun, get, go,
Gram, Gram's, gray, green, has, hat, hats,
huge, in, is, it, it's, left, let's, Mom, next,
nice, off, on, plan, playing, Pops, Rob, see,
sees, she, silk, snack, so, soft, takes, tan,
tells, then, things, this, trunk, up, vest,
wait, we, we'll, we're, when, will, with

High-Frequency Words
New
laugh, paper

Previously Taught
a, around, come, far,
have, I, looks, of, put,
puts, the, they've, to,
what, what's, where, you

Rex Knows

page 123

Decodable Words
Target Skill: Contractions *'ve, 're*
we're, we've

Target Skill: Vowel Pairs *oa, ow*
bowl, coat, Joan, knows, slow

Previously Taught Skills
and, as, asks, at, bell, brush, can, can't,
dog, Duke, each, eat, eats, feels, fills, fun,
get, gets, glad, go, he, him, hints, his,
in, is, it, it's, job, Kate, leash, lets, likes,
make, much, must, Nat, no, on, play,
playing, Rex, Rick, ring, rings, see, sees,
sits, smile, so, soft, stay, still, stop, stops,
tells, that, then, time, tricks, up, wake,
way, we, we'll, while, with, yes

High-Frequency Words
New
great, laugh, soon, talk,
they're, work

Previously Taught
a, do, down, for, friend,
good, have, her, I, our,
the, they're, to, too, you,
your

Bedtime for Ray

page 131

Decodable Words

Target Skill: Compound Words
bathtub, bedside, bedtime, weekday

Previously Taught Skills
8:00, and, as, at, be, bed, big, brush, but,
can, can't, dad, didn't, dream, game, get,
gets, go, grins, has, he, him, his, if, in, is,
it, last, let, lift, likes, must, nice, on, play,
Ray, Ray's, reads, rug, rule, see, Shep,
Shep's, six, sleep, sleeps, so, steps, tale,
teeth, tell, that, think, time, tub, up, went,
win, wins, with, yet

High-Frequency Words

New
mother, try, want,
wanted

Previously Taught
a, about, do, out, the, to,
was, watch, what, you

Pancake Ran

page 139

Decodable Words

Target Skill: Compound Words
cannot, hillside, pancake, roadside,
sailboat, sunrise, windmill

Previously Taught Skills
am, an, and, as, asked, at, big, boasted,
but, can, catch, close, did, Fox, get, Goat,
going, got, grunted, he, him, hissed, is,
it, jumped, just, made, Madge, me, met,
Midge, no, not, on, past, ran, rested,
sailed, sails, sat, Sheep, then, this, trip,
up, while, white, will, with, yelled

High-Frequency Words

New
door, old, try

Previously Taught
a, after, are, down, for,
hear, I, out, said, the,
where, you

171

A Springtime Rain

page 147

Decodable Words

Target Skill: Short Vowel /ĕ/ea
head, spread

Target Skill: Compound Words
pathways, playtime, rainbow, raincoat, raindrops, springtime, sunshine

Previously Taught Skills
and, as, be, Beth, Beth's, can, can't, class, clean, Dad, dog, dressed, fun, get, glad, glass, glows, grow, Gwen, hand, has, hat, he, helps, his, huge, in, is, it, its, it's, Jane, Kay, like, likes, long, lot, make, matching, mom, must, on, peeks, plants, quick, Quinn, rain, rains, see, sees, she, shine, slides, so, stay, swings, takes, them, this, up, use, way, we, wet, when, yells

High-Frequency Words

New
use, wash

Previously Taught
a, are, for, her, holds, looks, out, the, their, they, to, too, walk, watches, you

Rosebud

page 155

Decodable Words

Target Skill: Short Vowel /ĕ/ea
head, read, spread

Target Skill: Compound Words
bedtime, daytime, inside, paintbrushes, Rosebud, rosebud, sailboat, sunrise, sunset, topside

Previously Taught Skills
an, and, at, bed, being, big, boat, but, chose, day, days, fun, games, glowed, go, got, had, if, in, it, let, long, me, Mom, Mom's, name, nice, no, not, on, paint, painted, peeked, played, rained, rays, red, rocked, row, sail, sailed, sailing, sang, sea, set, sit, songs, stayed, sun, sun's, than, that, then, time, trip, up, we, we'd, went, when, white, yet

High-Frequency Words

New
more, mother, old

Previously Taught
a, all, I, my, one, out, sometimes, the, to, was, yellow, your